THE NATURE KIDS GUIDE TO

JACKRABBITS

DAVID ANDERSON

LP Media Inc. Publishing
Text copyright © 2026 by LP Media Inc.
All rights reserved.

For information address LP Media Inc. Publishing,
30012 Variolite St NW, Princeton MN 55371
www.lpmedia.org

Publication Data

Jackrabbits
The Nature Kid's Guide to Jackrabbits — First edition.

Summary: "Learn all about Jackrabbits, the Nature Kid Way"
— Provided by publisher.

ISBN: 979-8-89818-144-4

[1. Jackrabbits - Non-Fiction] I. Title.

Title: The Nature Kid's Guide to Jackrabbits

CONTENTS

DESERT LIFE

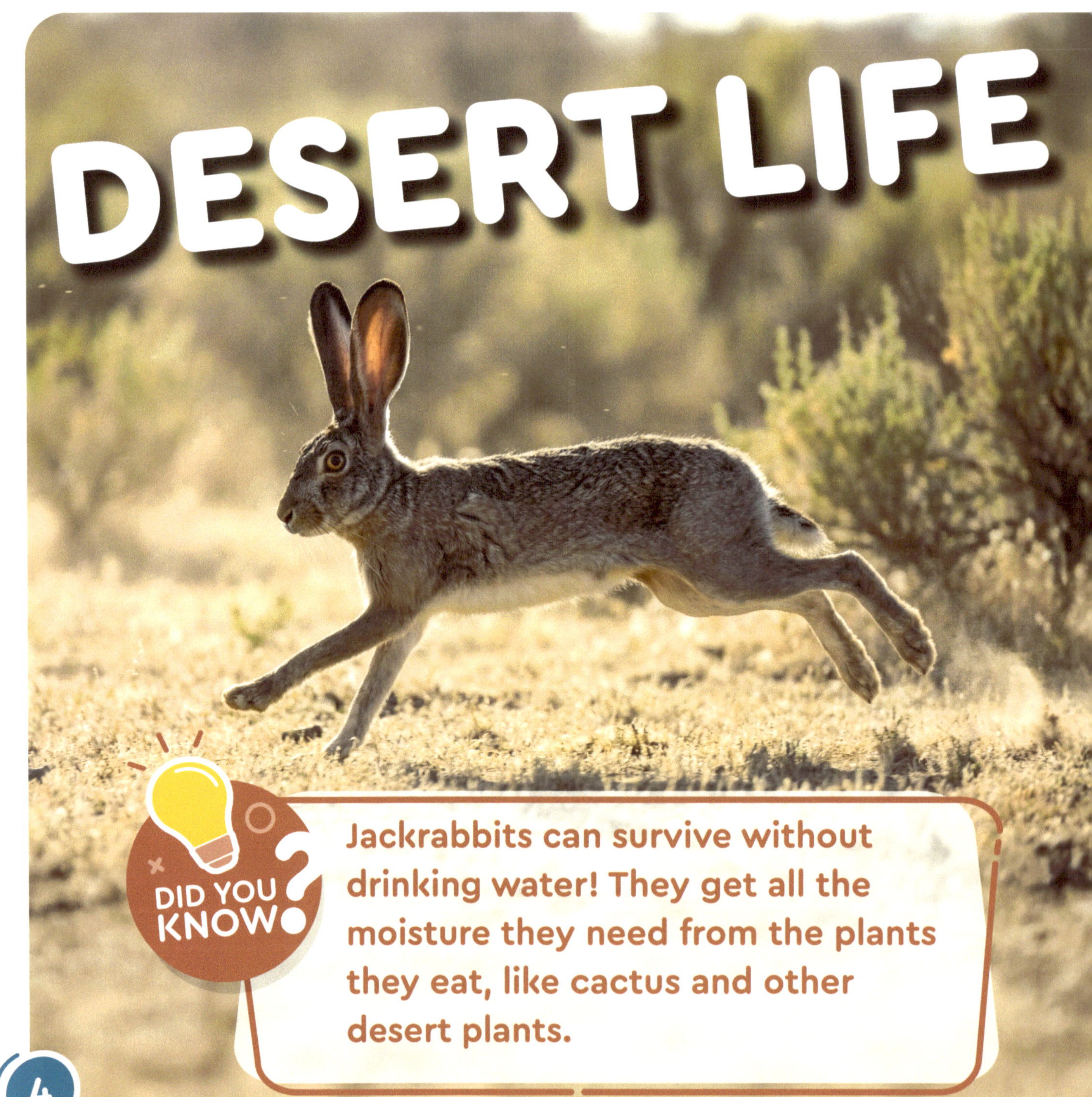

Jackrabbits can survive without drinking water! They get all the moisture they need from the plants they eat, like cactus and other desert plants.

Whoosh! A jackrabbit dashes across the hot sand. Its long ears stand tall.

Jackrabbits are not really rabbits. They are **hares**! Hares are similar to rabbits but have longer legs and bigger ears.

Jackrabbits got their name from their huge ears. People thought they looked like donkey ears, and male donkeys are called jacks.

Jackrabbits live in dry, open places. They make their homes in deserts and grasslands. Some live in scrubby areas with low bushes. They do not dig burrows like rabbits do.

These hares rest in shallow dips in the ground. They find shady spots under bushes to stay cool.

JACK MAP

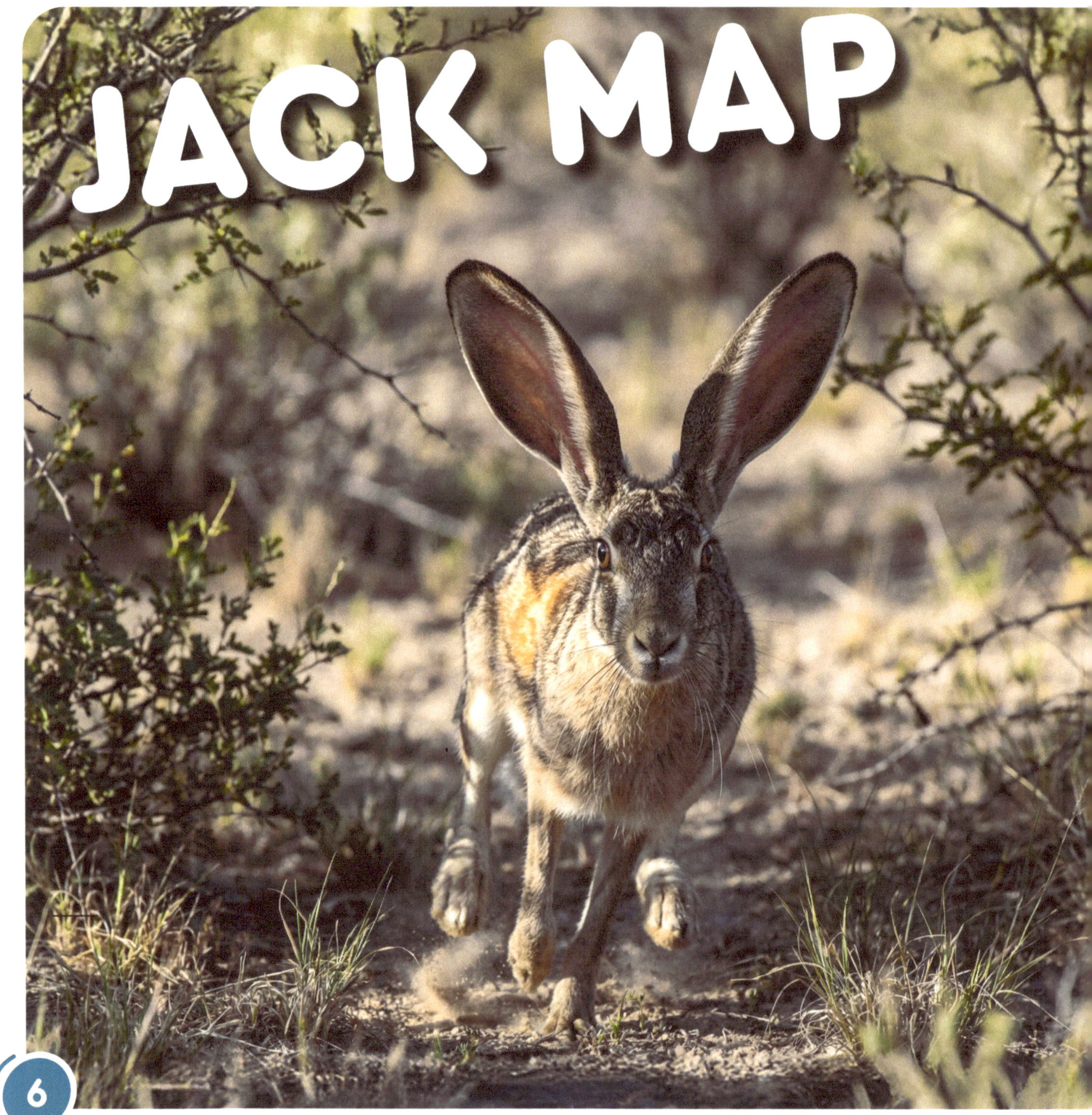

Thump! A jackrabbit runs through a hole in the bushes.

Jackrabbits live in North America. They roam from Canada to Mexico.

Black-tailed jackrabbits live in the western United States. They like hot, dry places. White-tailed jackrabbits live farther north. They like cool grasslands.

Antelope jackrabbits live in Arizona and Mexico. Each type has its own home.

A jackrabbit's ears can turn different ways. This helps it hear danger from all sides.

HOW BIG

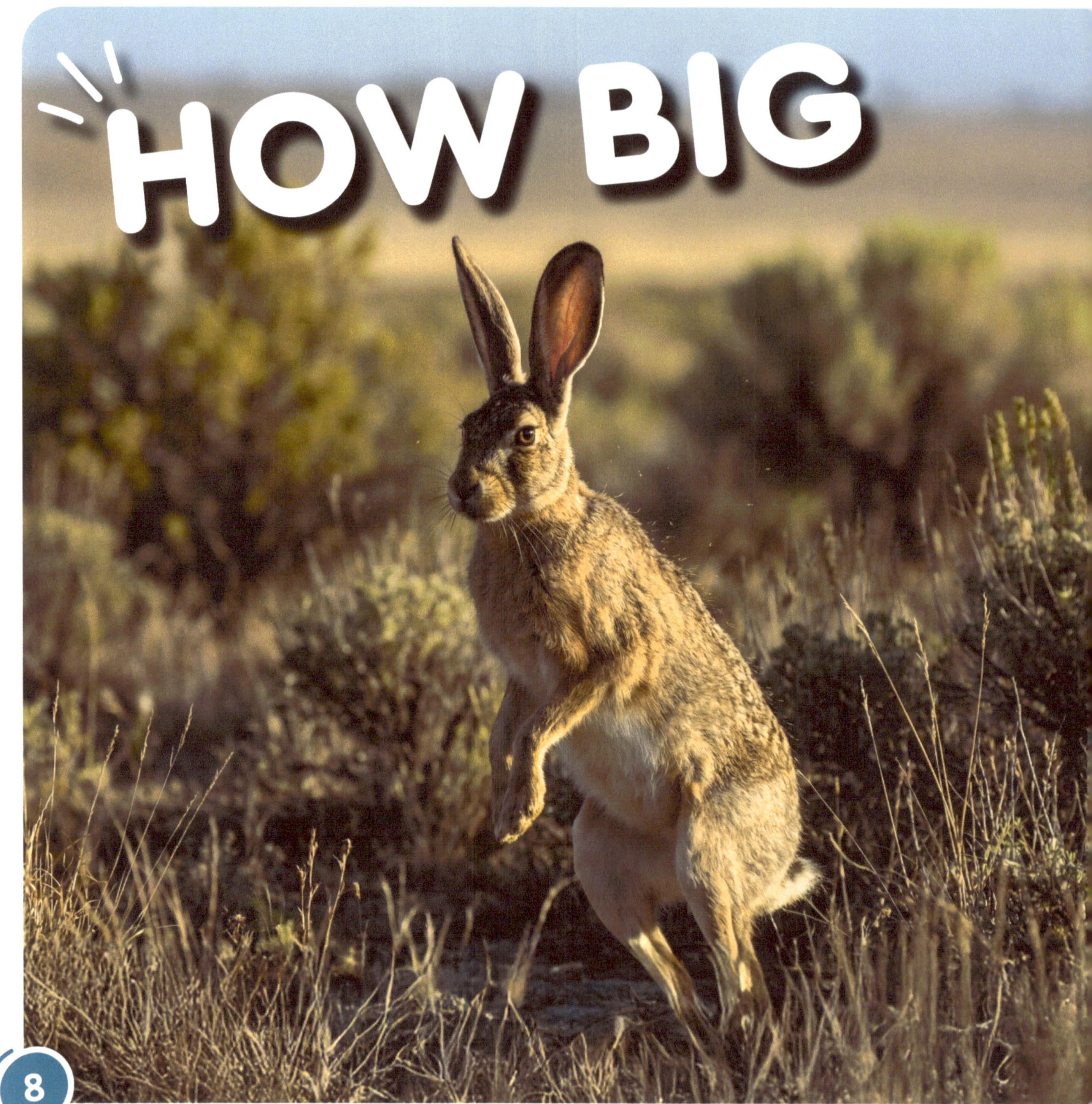

Snap! A jackrabbit stretches its long back legs. It sits up tall.

Jackrabbits are large hares. They can weigh 6 to 9 pounds. That is about as heavy as a cat.

Their bodies are 18 to 25 inches long. Their famous ears add 5 to 8 more inches! Their back legs are very long too, built for jumping. Those powerful legs can launch a jackrabbit 10 feet in a single leap!

Female jackrabbits are usually larger than males.

Unlike rabbits, hares are born with fur and already have their eyes open.

ENORMOUS EARS

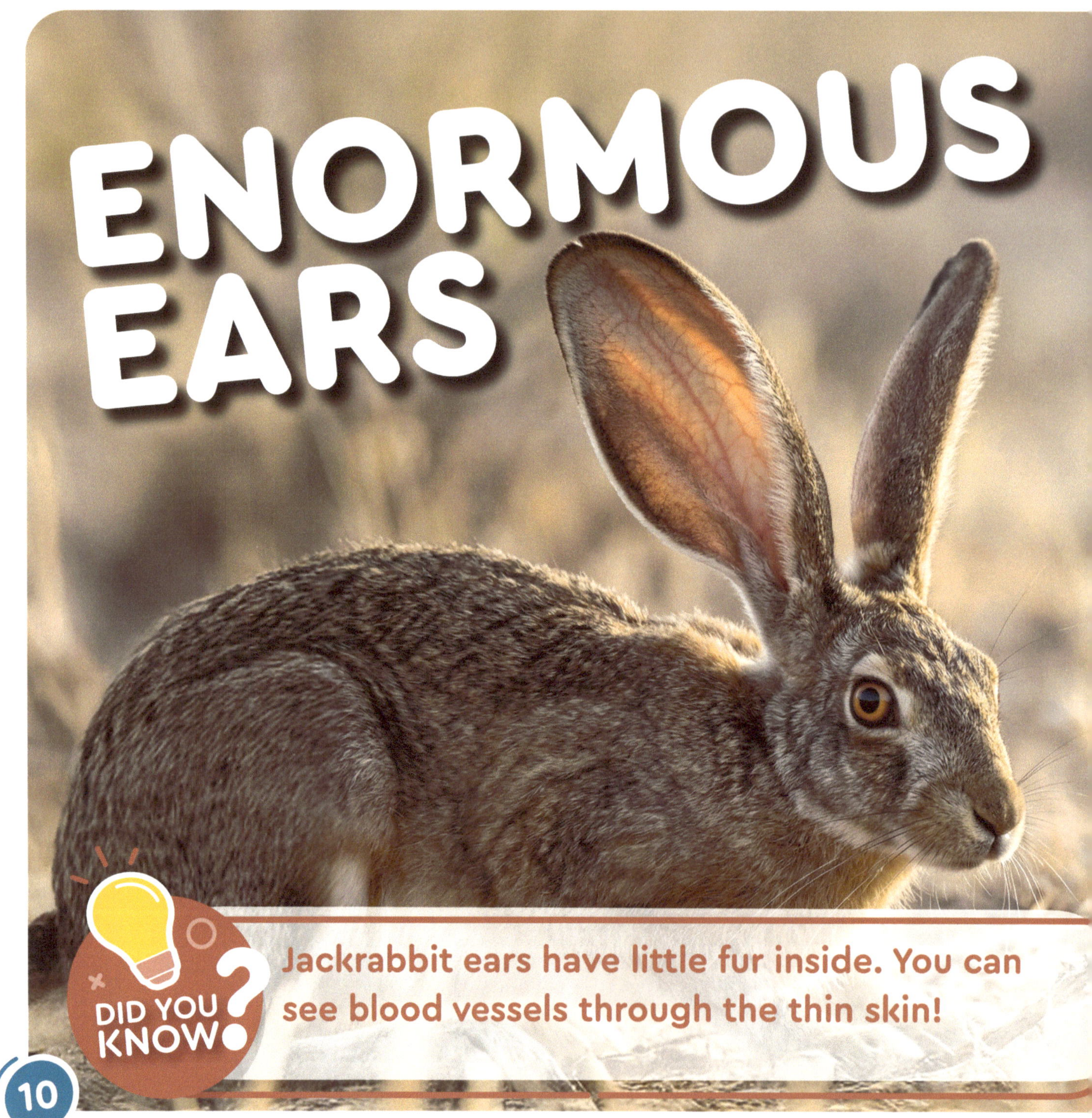

Jackrabbit ears have little fur inside. You can see blood vessels through the thin skin!

Twitch! A jackrabbit turns its huge ears. It listens closely.

Jackrabbit ears are amazing. They can be 8 inches long! That is almost one third of their whole body length.

Those big ears do two important jobs. They help Jackrabbits hear very well. This lets them catch sounds from all around.

The ears also keep jackrabbits cool on hot desert days. The ears have very thin skin with lots of blood flowing through. The big ears let heat escape from their bodies, like a built-in fan that is always running.

SUPER
SENSES

Wiggle! A jackrabbit freezes, its nose wiggling fast.

Jackrabbits have super senses. Their ears can hear sounds up to 2 miles away. They can turn each ear in a different direction!

Their big eyes sit on the sides of their head. This lets them see almost all around without moving.

Their nose never stops twitching. This helps them smell danger.

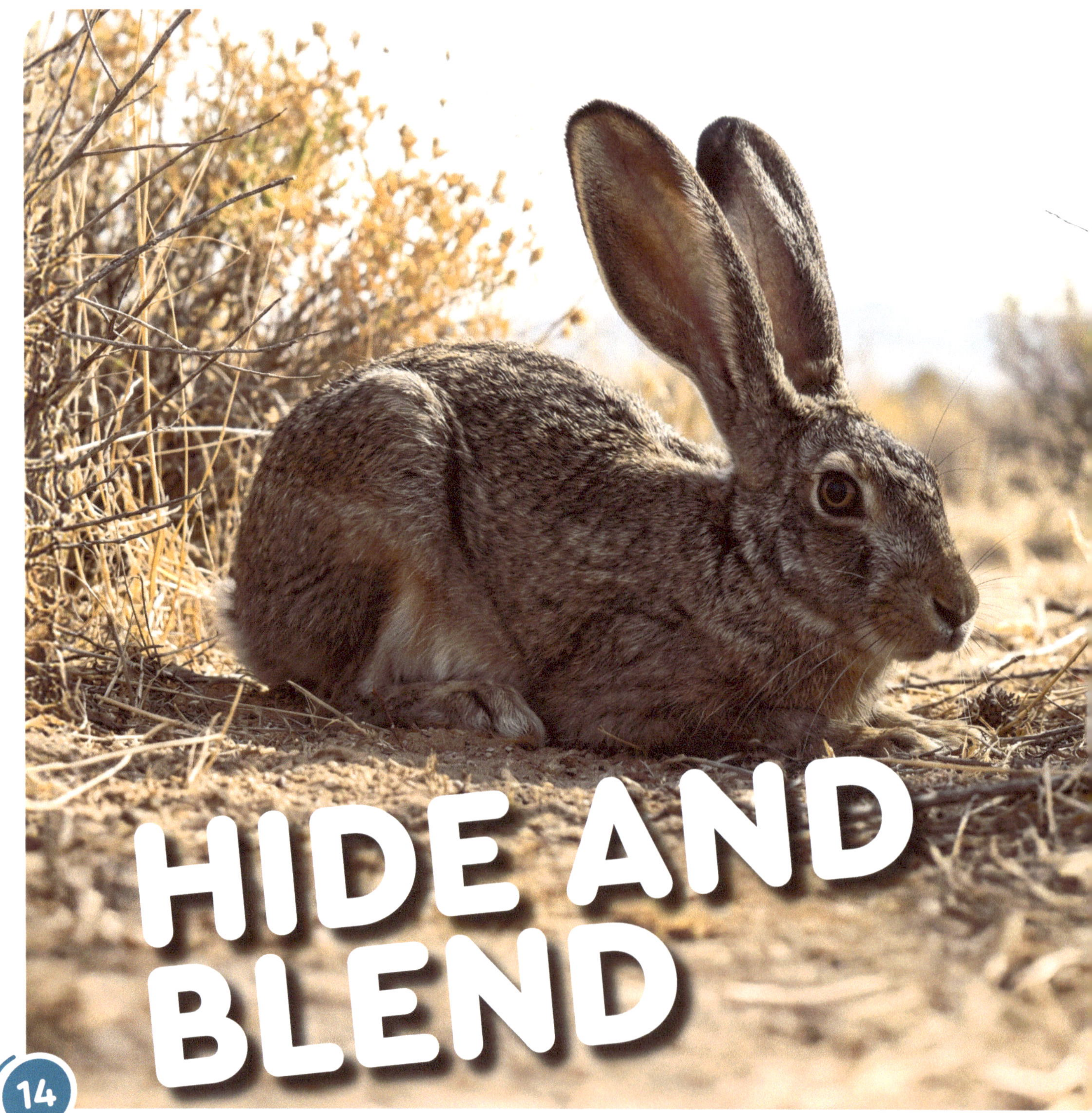

HIDE AND BLEND

Rustle! A jackrabbit crouches low in dry brush. It stays very still.

Jackrabbits are masters of hiding. Their fur matches the land around them. Brown and tan colors blend with dirt and dry grass.

This coloring is called **camouflage**. It helps Jackrabbits disappear from hungry eyes. Predators walk right past them!

Jackrabbits also stay very still when danger is near. They flatten their bodies against the ground.

DID YOU KNOW?

White-tailed jackrabbits change their fur to white in winter to match the snow.

16

Crunch! A jackrabbit nibbles on a cactus. Chewing keeps its teeth short.

Jackrabbits eat many kinds of plants. They munch on grasses, shrubs, and cacti. They can even eat prickly plants!

All these plants also give Jackrabbits water. They do not need to drink much because juicy stems and leaves give them all the water they need.

Jackrabbits eat at dawn and dusk. This is when it is cooler outside. They rest during the hot afternoon.

Jackrabbits can eat over one pound of plants each day!

THUMPING TALK

Stomp! A jackrabbit pounds the ground with its back foot.

Jackrabbits talk with their bodies. They do not use their voices much. Thumping is one way they send messages.

A jackrabbit senses danger. It thumps the ground hard. Other Jackrabbits feel the shaking. This tells them to watch out or run!

Jackrabbits use their ears too. Ears held back mean they are upset. Ears pointing forward mean they are alert.

Their tail sends messages too. When they run, the bright tail bobs up and down. This tells others to follow.

WATCH OUT

Screech! A hawk circles high above. A jackrabbit freezes.

Many animals hunt Jackrabbits. Hawks and eagles swoop down from the sky. They have sharp eyes that spot movement below.

Coyotes are another big threat. They chase Jackrabbits across the desert. Bobcats and foxes hunt them too.

Snakes also eat young Jackrabbits. Rattlesnakes hide and wait for them to pass by. At night, owls take over the hunt.

Golden eagles can dive at speeds of up to 200 miles per hour to catch prey!

ZOOM AWAY

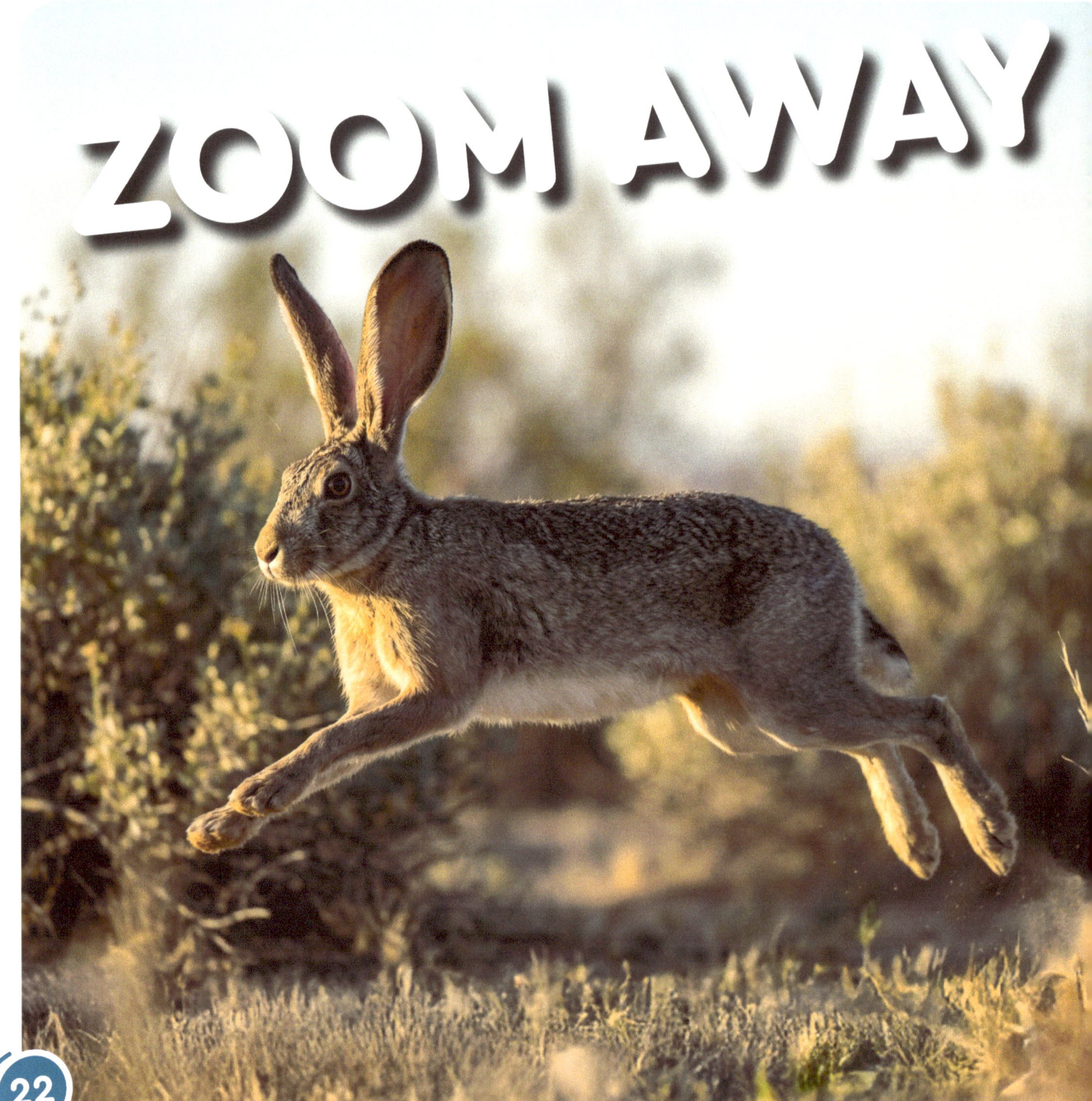

Zoom! A jackrabbit runs away. Its legs move so fast!

Jackrabbits are good at getting away. They run from danger. They do not fight.

Their back legs are strong. They push off fast. Jackrabbits can run 40 miles per hour. Their speed keeps them safe.

They also zigzag when they run. This tricks the animals chasing them and makes them hard to follow as they dart through the brush.

LEAPING
LEGS

Spring! A jackrabbit leaps high into the air and bounds away.

Jackrabbits have amazing legs built for jumping. Their back legs are much longer than their front legs, which gives them extra power.

These strong legs help them leap far. One jump can cover up to 20 feet of ground! That is longer than a car.

Jackrabbits hop on their toes. This helps them push off fast.

Jackrabbits can reach full hopping speed in just three bounds from a standstill!

DAY AND NIGHT

Hoot! An owl flies overhead. Below, a jackrabbit hides until dawn.

Jackrabbits are most active at dawn and dusk. That means they are **crepuscular**, and the desert is cooler then.

During the hot day, Jackrabbits rest in the shade. They find cool spots under bushes or in shallow dips in the ground.

At night, they may come out to eat. The darkness also helps keep them safe from some predators.

Jackrabbits have special eyes that see well in low light. They can see best at twilight time!

LONER LIFE

Squeak! A jackrabbit sits alone. It watches the desert.

Jackrabbits sometimes feed in groups to watch for danger, but they do not share food or live together. Each jackrabbit takes care of itself.

This means they do not have families like some other animals. Each one finds its own food and shelter.

Sometimes several jackrabbits might be around each other. But they are not a team.

Jackrabbits do not dig burrows. Instead, they rest in shallow dips called forms.

BOXING
HARES

Pow! Two Jackrabbits stand on their back legs. They box with their paws.

Jackrabbits box during mating season. They stand up tall and swat at each other with their front paws. This looks like a boxing match!

Females often box males to test their strength. A female may hit a male that gets too close.

In warm climates, jackrabbits can breed year-round. This means they may box in any season when food is easy to find.

Boxing matches between jackrabbits can last up to an hour, with breaks between rounds!

LITTLE LEVERETS

Chirp! A tiny baby jackrabbit sits still. Its eyes are wide open.

Baby Jackrabbits are called **leverets**. They are born with fur and open eyes. This helps them survive in the wild right away.

A mother jackrabbit can have up to six leverets at one time. She may have several litters each year.

Leverets can hop just hours after birth. They hide in grass and stay very quiet to stay safe. When they are about two weeks old, leverets start eating plants.

GROWING UP

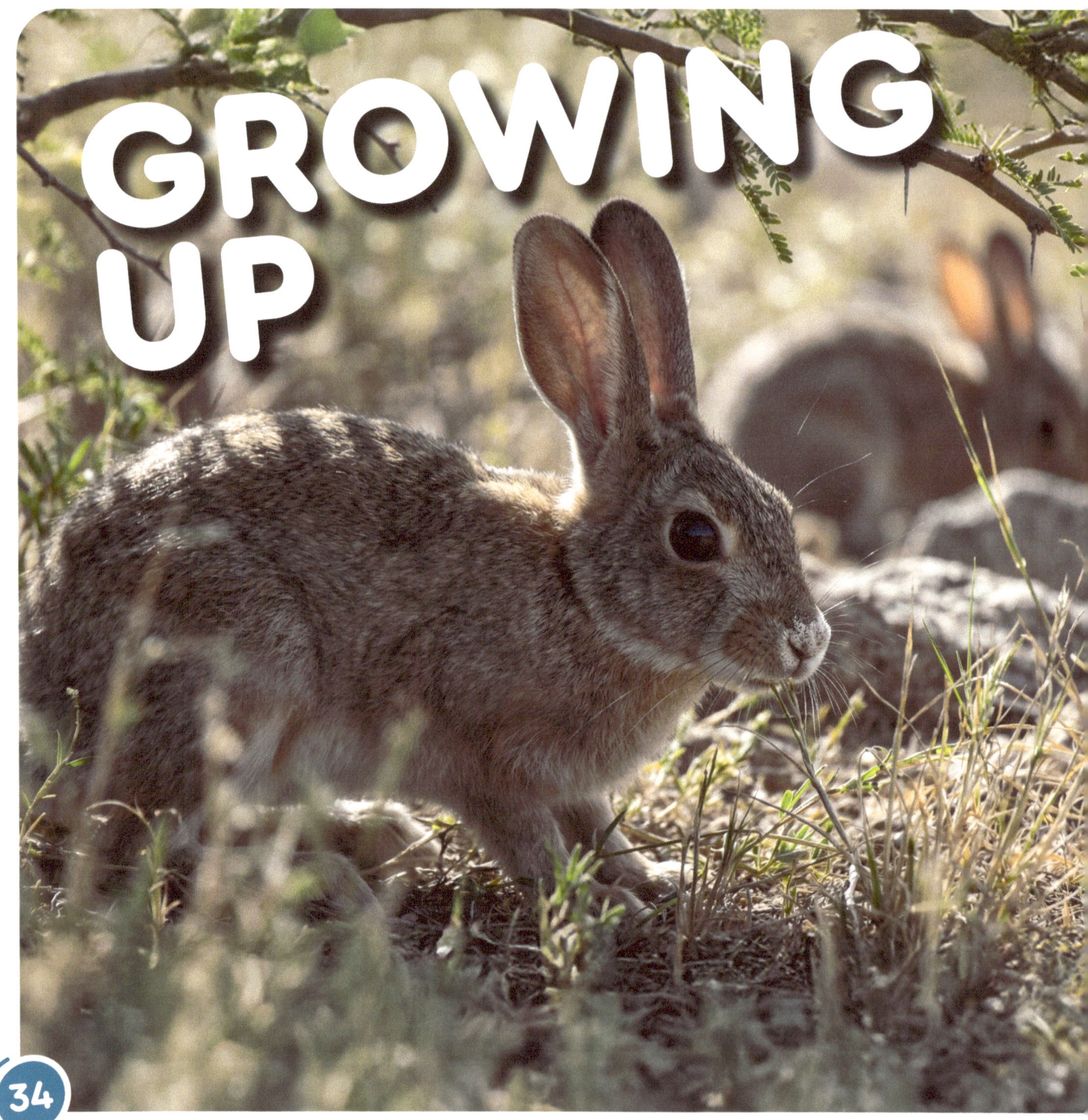

Snort! A young jackrabbit nibbles grass. This leveret is growing fast.

Leverets grow up quickly. They do not stay with their mother for long. After about one month, leverets are ready to live on their own.

Mother Jackrabbits visit their babies only once or twice a day. They come at night to feed them milk. This keeps **predators** from finding the hiding spot.

By one month old, young Jackrabbits look like small adults. They can run fast and find their own food.

A leveret can outrun a person by the time it is one month old!

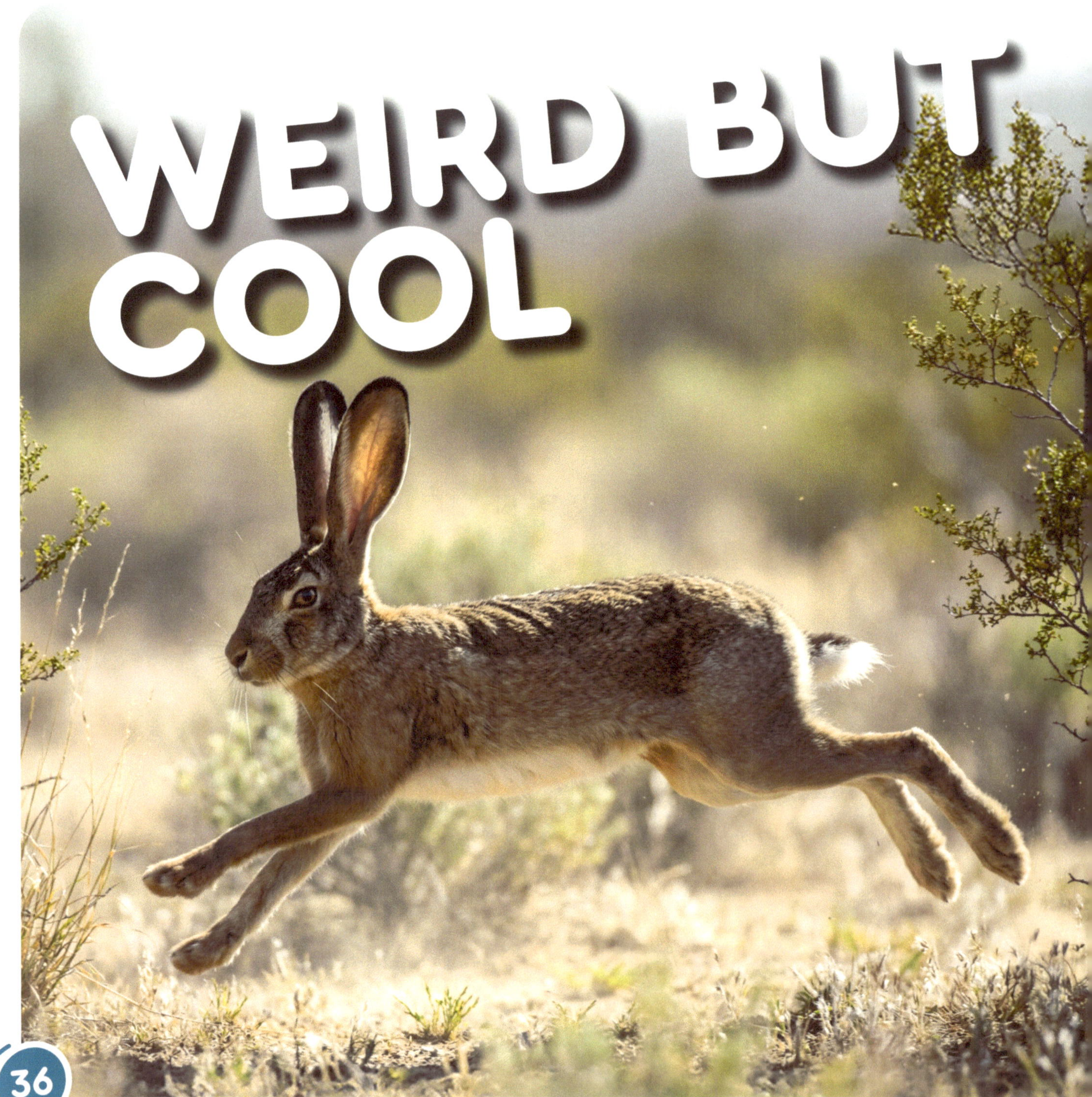

WEIRD BUT COOL

Jackrabbits have some strange tricks hidden inside their bodies!

A jackrabbit skull has tiny holes all over it. It looks like a honeycomb! These holes work like shock absorbers. They cushion each landing when the jackrabbit hops.

Here is a gross one. Jackrabbits eat their food twice! They make special droppings full of vitamins. Then they eat the droppings to get more nutrition from their food. Desert plants are tough and dry, so this helps them survive.

Jackrabbits cannot throw up... ever! A strong muscle in their throat only lets food go down, never up.

HARE SPOTTING

Bring binoculars! Jackrabbits feel safer when you stay far back, so you will see more if you keep your distance.

Look! Somethings moving behind that sage brush. It's a jackrabbit!

Want to spot a jackrabbit? Here are some tips!

Go outside at dawn or dusk. This is when jackrabbits are most active. Look in open fields, desert areas, or grassy spots near bushes.

Stay quiet and move slowly. Jackrabbits have amazing hearing and will run if you are loud. Crouch down low and watch from far away.

Look for their big ears first. The ears often stick up above the grass. You might also see them sitting very still, hoping you will not notice them.

GLOSSARY

hares
Animals that look like rabbits but have longer legs and bigger ears.

camouflage
Colors or patterns that help an animal hide by matching what is around it.

predators
Animals that hunt and eat other animals.

crepuscular
Active during dawn and dusk when the sun is low.

leverets
Baby hares that are born with fur and open eyes.